Lenny

in
Paris

The perfect

French menu

for your next

cocktail soirée

B.G. Gordon

Arc Light Books
Portland, Oregon

savor the time
spent with friends

make delicious memories

Lenny in Paris is an homage to my companion Lenny, a citizen of the world who had a passion for fine cuisine.

A Hollywood dog, Lenny was brought up surrounded by titans of film, art, theater, and – of course – the restaurant world.

These classic french bistro recipes will always remind me of the summer Lenny and I spent together on our quest through Paris.

I hope this photo journal of our adventures in Paris inspires you to live and cook like a Parisian.

So, put on a beret and invite your friends over for a soirée. Lenny and I will walk you through everything you need to make the evening a success!

Cook Like an Artiste

Cooking, like painting, requires a touch of magic and a spirit
of improvisation. We mix in nature's elements, and when
combined, we awaken layers of scents and flavors greater
than the sum of their parts. Lenny in Paris walks you
through basic French recipes from Lenny and my favorite
Bistro experiences. Enclosed you will find an assortment
of condiments and hors d'oeuvres that can be mixed
and matched to your guests' delight.

A little French music, one or two of these savory
hors d'oeuvres, a sweet dessert, and a potion
is the perfect recipe for a gathering of friends.

Bon appétit

soirée menu

Condiments

grapefruit marmalade
Dijon mustard
mayonnaise
herb salad
crème fraîche

Hors d'oeuvres

pissaladière
salt cod brandade
chicken liver pâté
steak tartare
caviar pie

Desserts

poached pears with roquefort
pot de crème with chantilly crème
vacherin with berries
champagne cocktail, kir and kir royal
café cognac
lavender hot chocolate with chantilly crème

Grapefruit Marmalade

4 ruby red grapefruits

6 tbsp lemon juice

2 cups sugar

2 cups brown sugar

In a large pot, place the 4 grapefruit in just enough water to make them float freely. Bring to a boil and let boil for two hours (add water from a kettle if too much boils away so the grapefruit doesn't touch the bottom).

Drain the grapefruit, and discard water letting the fruit cool (or else you'll burn your hands!).

Slice the grapefruit as finely as possible, removing seeds and any tough membrane.

Chop finely. Take your time to chop well. It doesn't have to be uniform. Put the grapefruit, sugars and lemon juice back into the pot, and dissolve the sugars on low heat. Bring to a boil and let bubble until you reach the gel point, about 15 minutes, give-or-take.

If you like a smoother consistency, blend in food processor for a bit until you get the consistency you like. Ladle into clean sterilized jars and process in a hot water bath for ten minutes.

Makes 10 servings and a lovely gift to bring to the host when you are invited to their soirée.

Wonderful on croissant, breads, pastry, glaze for duck and chicken, as well as a sweetener for your tea.

I like to add a drop of rose geranium flower oil inside, it adds a mysterious and magical flavor for a complex palate.

Voilà!

Dijon Mustard

2 cups dry white wine or champagne

1 large onion,chopped

3 garlic cloves, minced

1 cup mustard powder or ground mustard seeds

3 tbsp honey

1 tbsp safflower or canola oil

2 tsp salt

In saucepan combine wine, onion and garlic. Heat to a boil. Simmer 5 minutes and strain all solids.

Cool and set aside.

Whisk in dry mustard powder or grind your own mustard seeds into a powder.

Sprinkle into cooked liquid and stir in honey, oil, and salt, stirring constantly. Pour into glass jar and cool at room temperature overnight.

Refrigerate and age for 2 weeks before serving.

Leave seeds whole for rustic style, gets better with age... like we do.

Mayonnaise

2 fresh farm egg yolks

1 tsp Dijon mustard

4 tsp lemon juice

1 cup safflower oil

1 pinch of coarse salt and ground pepper to taste

In a blender or food processor put in egg yolks, Dijon mustard, and lemon juice (or whisk by hand).

Turn on blender and add oil in a steady stream until the mixture starts to thicken.

Once it's a thick emulsion, add salt and pepper or if you like spice, try adding Tabasco

Refrigerate in an airtight container and it will last up to 1week and If you like spice, try adding Tabasco

Try customizing with herbs and spices like paprika, garlic, or tarragon. It's delicious on steak and potatoes!

Always make from scratch, it's worth it.

Crème Fraîche

1 cup heavy cream

⅓ cup buttermilk

Add heavy cream into a sterile container add buttermilk and whisk together.

Place on in a warm place in your kitchen, perhaps above your stove for 2 days until it sets to a thick consistency.

Cover and chill in the refrigerator and you have the most delicious sour cream to serve on your desserts and savory snacks

You will never buy sour cream again.

Herb Salad

parsley	celery tips
chives	shallots
tarragon	lemon
chervil	olive oil
baby arugula	fleur de sel

Carefully pick the leaves from all the fresh herbs, slicing the chives and shallots. Combine in a bowl with a squeeze of lemon and drizzle of olive oil toss and sprinkle with fleur de sel.

You wouldn't believe the delightful layers of flavors when added to your hors d'oeuvres

Pissaladière

caramelized onion tart

12 medium yellow onions, thinly sliced

4   sprigs thyme

2   bay leaves

4   ancho whole dried chilies

1   cup pitted, halved black olives

1   jar oil-packed anchovies, drained

1   package frozen puff pastry dough

Chop onions in small slices. Break them up in a roasting pan
tossing in bay leaf, and leaves of thyme. Add 2 ancho chilies
whole, (for heat) and place in oven at 350. Tossing every
10 minutes. When softened and clear lower oven to 250
and cook slowly for 2 hours, constantly stirring till a golden
brown onion jelly. No oil or butter needed if cooked long and
slow at low heat.

This will draw out the sugar in the onions making it incredibly delicious on its own. The alchemy
of the onion is magic! It can be used in many recipes in this form and can be jarred like jelly.
When cooled, it can be frozen for future use and it will last for months in the freezer.

Lay parchment paper on cookie sheet to place pastry. Roll out puff pastry dough and
on floured surface and use floured rolling pin just enough to smooth dough to your desired size.

Brandade

salt cod mashed potatoes

1 pound skinless, boneless salt cod

2 cups milk

1 large thyme sprig

1 bay leaf

5 peppercorns

2 allspice berries

1 whole clove

1 pound potatoes, peeled, cut 1-inch cubes

6 large garlic cloves, peeled

1 cup olive oil

1 pinch salt and pepper

1 pinch cayenne pepper

1 pinch grated nutmeg

½ tsp grated lemon zest

¾ cup crème fraîche

3 tbsp cold butter

1 can plum tomatoes

Rinse salt cod well, rub off any salt and soak in 2 quarts cold water, or drain changing water every few hours (an overnight soak without changing is fine). Total soaking time should be at least 8 hours.

In a medium saucepan, heat milk over medium-high heat. Add soaked salt cod, thyme, bay leaf, peppercorns, allspice berries and clove. Adjust heat to maintain a bare simmer. Cook until fish flakes easily, about 15 minutes. Remove fish from milk bath set aside and keep at room temperature.

In another pot, cover potatoes with water and bring to a boil. Add garlic cloves and a good pinch of salt. Drain potatoes when they are soft, about 15 minutes. Put potatoes in a large mixing bowl. With your fingers, flake cooked salt cod on top. With a potato masher, roughly blend potatoes and fish. Warm the garlic that was boiled with potatoes in 1 cup olive oil. Use half of the garlic oil drizzled into mixture and mash again. Add cayenne, nutmeg to taste and lemon zest , along with crème fraîche at the end to thicken to a rich mashed potato paste.

Heat oven to 400 degrees. In your baking dish or pie pan, place a layer canned plum tomatoes on bottom and roast tomatoes for 10 minutes to concentrate flavor of tomato. Transfer brandade mixture over tomatoes smoothing with a spatula covering it completely and drizzle with remaining garlic oil and bake. Bake until golden and bubbling, about 15 to 20 minutes.

Serve with Baguette toasts for digging down to the tomato at the bottom.
Very nice with a deep red wine.

Chicken Liver Pâté

1   pound fresh organic chicken livers, cleaned

1   stick cold unsalted butter, cut into pieces

½ cup cubed chopped bacon

1   minced garlic clove

1   cup chopped yellow onions

1   dash ground cloves

1   dash ground nutmeg

1   dash cayenne pepper

1   dash dried coriander

1   dash dried marjoram

1   dash dried basil

1   dash dried rosemary

1   dash dried thyme

1   dash dried tarragon

2   bay leaves

¼ tsp salt

¼ tsp freshly ground black pepper

½ cup Calvados apple brandy

½ cup heavy cream

In a skillet, sauté bacon pieces till lightly brown remove and set aside bacon. Leaving bacon grease in pan, add a tablespoon of butter to bacon fat and sauté onions and garlic until soft. When onions are soft add livers and pinch of each herb together and sauté in fat until golden brown on both sides about 3 minutes each side, livers should be pink on the inside and tender. Discard the bay leaves, and cool slightly.

Pour warm ingredients into food processor but before blending add Calvados brandy to skillet and de glaze the juices and add to the food processor. Add remaining chilled butter cubes and blend until creamy. Place in a mixing bowl and let cool and fold in heavy cream until combined. Place in ramekins for serving and refrigerate until firm, at least 6 hours.

Serve with toasted French baguette, cornichons (baby pickles), herb salad and Dijon mustard.

Refrigerate until firm, at least 6 hours.

Champagne, red, or a lovely dry rosé wine for a potion.

All are a perfect compliment.

INTERDIT
AUX CHIENS

DEFENSE DE FUMER

Régionaux

Produits

14	oz center cut beef or fresh venison tenderloin trimmed of fat
1½	tbsp Dijon mustard
2	tbsp mayonnaise
6	tbsp salt packed capers rinsed then minced
2	tbsp minced parsley
1	small shallot finely chopped
1½	tsp Worcestershire sauce
¼	tsp Tabasco sauce
1	farm fresh egg (optional)

Use the highest quality beef filet tenderloin from your butcher, or even better a fresh tenderloin of venison.

Place in the freezer for 10 minutes before chopping to make firm and keep cold.

Take out of the freezer and chop it by hand with a sharp knife in small fine pieces and combine in a bowl with, mustard, mayonnaise, minced the capers, parsley, shallots and add Worcestershire sauce and Tabasco for heat(optional). Salt and pepper to taste.

Serve with toasted baguette slices and mixed herb salad.

A good red wine is always a complement to the fine choice of beef.

Champagne or Champagne cocktail can make it extra special.

Fit for a King.
Ç'est Magnifique!

Caviar Pie

Elle's Caviar Pie

2 jars black roe Caviar
1 cup crème fraîche
1 small sweet onion
8 hard boiled eggs
1 cup mayonnaise

Layered from bottom up, in a tart pie dish:

8 hard boiled egg chopped fine & mixed
with mayonnaise,

1 finely chopped sweet onion layered over egg,

crème fraîche spread evenly over chopped onion,

Caviar layered over crème fraîche,

Garnish with finely chopped parsley
and lemon wedge.

Serve with toasted baguette slices.

New Year's Eve and Christmas are the perfect
celebrations to make this delight.

Champagne Cocktail Please!

Poached Pears with Roquefort

1   Blue Cheese wedge

6   large pears

1   bottle white table wine

¾ cup of sugar

1   cinnamon stick

1   lemon

1   vanilla bean slice lengthwise

4   peppercorns

4   cloves

1   cup red balsamic vinegar

Peel the pear skin with vegetable peeler
leaving stem at top. Place in deep stew pot
made of enamel or stainless steel. Add the pears,
cinnamon stick vanilla bean (cut in half),
lemon, (cut in half), sugar, peppercorns and cloves.

Cover contents in pot with white wine.
On a medium flame, bring to a boil.
Turn to a simmer for another 20 minutes.
Let cool in wine bath.

In a separate small saucepan heat balsamic vinegar
on a low flame and stir until it thickens into a syrup
for about five minutes.

Serve a whole pear with chunk of Roquefort cheese
and drizzle with balsamic syrup

Perfect with a glass of rosé or Champagne Cocktail

A Poem

Chocolate Pot de Crème

3 dark 70 % chocolate bars

1 egg

1 cup scorched milk

1 tsp vanilla

1 shot Chambord Liqueur (or whiskey)

In a blender, add chocolate bars broken in pieces, with an egg, vanilla, and a shot of liqueur or whiskey.

While blending contents, pour scorching hot milk through top hole of blender.

Blend till completely smooth, about 1 minute.

Pour into 4 miniature souffle dessert cups and let set in the refrigerator about 3 hours.

Serve with fresh berries or plain, but defiantly with Chantilly Crème on top!

My dear friend Keith's recipe.

Chantilly Crème

2 cups heavy cream

1 tsp vanilla

1 tbsp sugar

In a chilled bowl, add heavy cream, vanilla and sugar. Whisk by hand or mixer, until ingredients form a cloud of soft cream. Be sure not to whisk to much, or you will have butter.

Dolloped on top of your Pot de Crème, and just about everything and anything.

Filling

2 cups crème fraîche
2 pints of fresh berries
⅓ cup of sugar
Juice of one lemon

the oven off leaving oven door cracked open, while meringue cools in the oven.

In a separate bowl, stir berries with sugar and lemon juice.
And so the juices emerge.

Peel meringue from parchment carefully. Place on lovely serving platter. Crack open the top of the meringue making a well in center and dollop crème fraîche inside the well. Cover crème fraîche with the macerated berries and finally a layer of Chantilly Crème.

The fine art
of flavors and textures.

A Masterpiece!

Champagne Cocktail

4 drops of bitters   1 twist of lemon

1 sugar cube   1 ounce of Cognac (optional)

Drop a sugar cube in the bottom of your flute glass, dripping bitters over the sugar cube.

Pour in Cognac, and add your champagne. To complete, twist a slice of lemon rind over the top to add the oil of lemon and drop inside (cherry optional). Add Champagne slowly.

To refresh, continue to add chilled Champagne.

Kir

Chilled dry white table wine with Crème de Cassis

Pour a glass of white wine. Drizzle a tablespoon amount of the Crème de Cassis inside. Crème de Cassis is a delicious potion of black currants from Dijon France and will make a reddish pink layer at the bottom of your glass, and as you sip you get the two flavors combined in your mouth. A potion of earth's fruits, the grape, and the berry!

Kir Royale

Chilled Champagne, instead of white wine, with Crème de Cassis.

Pour champagne in your favorite style champagne glass, then drizzle the Crème de Casis slowly inside. It will sink to the bottom giving the same layered effect, as you sip your bubbly it will blend into a lovely potion... tickling your nose.

Café Cognac

1   fresh brewed black coffee
    or espresso

1   oz cognac of your choice:
    Benedictine Brandy or
    Grand Marnier

1   dollop Chantilly Crème

Brew your coffee very strong,

or make it a double espresso.

Use honey or sugar to sweeten if you like.

Add a shot of cognac to your coffee
and top with Chantilly Crème.

Or your cognac can be served in a proper
cognac glass separately to be sipped
with your coffee.

This potion is nicely matched with a Chocolate Pot de Crème dessert.

Served alone, it is always a perfect ending to your soirée
and the finale of your gathering.

Lavender Hot Chocolate

Makes 4 servings

4 cups of milk or almond milk

1 bar of dark solid chocolate

1 tbsp of Lavender buds

1 (drop of rose water optional)

1 dollop of Chantilly Crème

In a saucepan on a low flame, warm your
milk and sprinkle in broken pieces of chocolate.

Whisk milk and dark chocolate till dissolved.
While this is all being combined, add the purple
flowers of Lavender to your mixture.

They will float on top as the milk heats up.
Taste and add more chocolate if needed.

When milk starts to boil the slightest bit, take it
off the flame and use a sieve to pour the potion
through to remove the flowers.

Serve in a demitasse cup with a dollop of Chantilly Crème and voilà!
Lavender Hot Cocoa can be an erotic potion.

Best just before bed, or on a rainy day.

Add dark rum or whiskey for that little extra something.

A most delicious way to end your evening, Sweet Dreams!

Every meal,
gathering, and party,
– like a film –
deserves a soundtrack
all its own
to heighten the senses
and to set the tone.

For this perfectly
Parisian soirée,
we suggest
the lilting melodies
of Charles Trenet
and Édith Piaf

Finis

A Vôtre Santé

special thanks
to my friends

Gary Glaser
James Hayes
Chef Corina Weibel
and Kevin

A classically trained fine artist, world traveler, and foodie, B.G. Gordon has spent
more than four decades working in the circus-like atmosphere of the theater
and film industry. After years of building and creating costumes and sets, a
Hollywood career began to take her around the world — and she didn't travel
alone. Lenny, her beloved canine companion, was quite the globe trotter.
Artists, chefs, muppet makers, good friends, and, yes — movie stars — have
all played a role in making this book a reality. More than just a compilation
of recipes, "Lenny in Paris" is a love letter to all who played a part, and of course
to the incomparable Lenny. In addition to this photo and recipe homage, there
is a video poem at www.youtube.com/watch?v=xU89JcJjQ4Y&t=2s,
titled: "Le Cimetiere Des Chiens - Paris Dog Cemetary."

Please enjoy.

CPSIA information can be obtained
at www.ICGtesting.com
Printed in the USA
BVHW061123250122
627119BV00010B/957

9781939353290